IS THERE REALLY BURIED TREASURE?

Contents

Written by Jillian Powell

Collins

T0321626

Is there really buried treasure?

Buried treasure does exist and there's still lots to be discovered!

Often treasure is found using a metal detector which bleeps when it detects something metal under the ground.

What is treasure?

Treasure can mean anything that someone values, because it's old or precious or just means a lot to them. Most treasure **troves** include gold and silver coins, jewellery or precious objects.

Roman coins

Objects that are important to our history and culture, including those made from gold and silver, or that contain precious metals and are over 300 years old, all count as treasure.

This gold and silver cup was found buried in a field in Yorkshire, UK, and it's over 1,000 years old.

How do people find buried treasure?

Some people find treasure by accident when they're digging for something else. In 1840, workers in Yorkshire repairing a riverbank dug up 7,500 Viking silver coins buried in a lead chest. In Suffolk, a metal detectorist looking for a farmer's lost hammer in 1992 discovered a rich **hoard** of Roman treasure.

Viking gold from the Cuerdale Hoard, Yorkshire, UK

Archaeologists are professional treasure hunters!
They're **historical** experts who search areas which
could contain buried treasure that will further our
understanding of the history of that place. They use
old maps and **aerial** or **artificial satellite** images to
help them look for treasure.

an archaeologist at work

What's the most valuable treasure ever found?

The richest hoard of Roman treasure ever found in Britain was buried in a field in Suffolk. The Hoxne Hoard contained over 15,000 gold and silver coins, as well as jewellery and decorative objects. Today, it's worth over 3.5 million pounds.

The largest hoard of Anglo-Saxon gold, silver and jewellery was found buried in a field in Staffordshire, UK, in 2009. There were over 3,500 items, and the hoard is worth over 3.2 million pounds today.

The value of hoards isn't just in how much money they're worth, they also have a lot of historical importance.

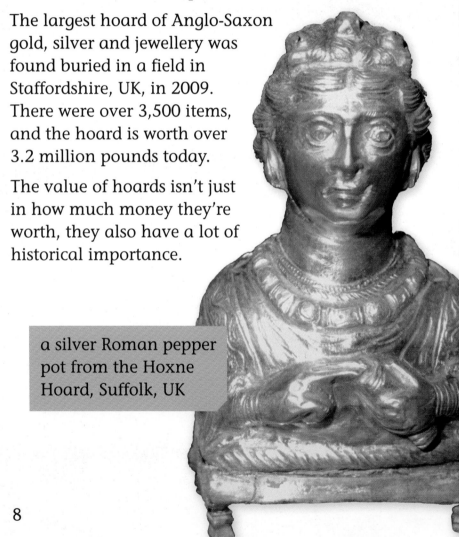

a silver Roman pepper pot from the Hoxne Hoard, Suffolk, UK

Why do people bury treasure?

People bury treasure to keep it safe. The Hoxne Hoard was buried at a time when the Romans **occupied** Britain and may have been hidden from Saxons, **Angles** and other **raiders**. The Staffordshire Hoard was buried by Saxons to hide it from Viking invaders.

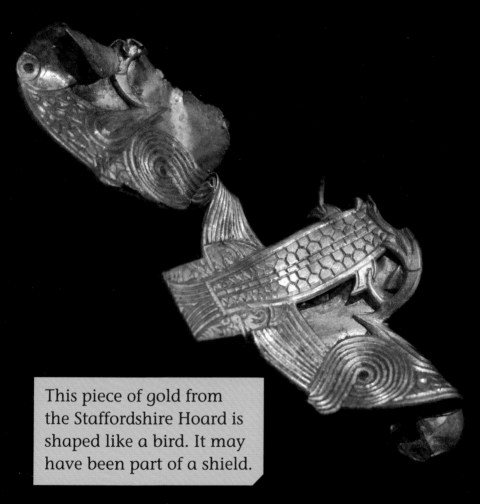

This piece of gold from the Staffordshire Hoard is shaped like a bird. It may have been part of a shield.

Where else do people find treasure?

Around three million shipwrecks are believed to lie under the world's oceans and rivers, some carrying treasure.

In 2015, divers spotted a group of gold coins lying on the seabed by the port of Caesarea on the Mediterranean Sea. Archaeologists found over 2,500 gold coins, bronze statues and objects from a trading ship which sank around 900 years ago.

a diver recovering gold coins from the seabed

Is there really pirate treasure?

There are many legends of lost pirate treasure, like the Treasure of Lima, stolen in 1820 by a dishonest ship's captain on the journey from Peru to Mexico. Legend says the treasure lies buried on Cocos Island in the Pacific, but no one has found it yet.

The *Whydah* was a pirate ship which sank off the coast of Cape Cod, USA, in 1717. On board was treasure stolen from more than 50 other ships, including over 15,000 gold and silver coins, African jewellery and belt buckles.

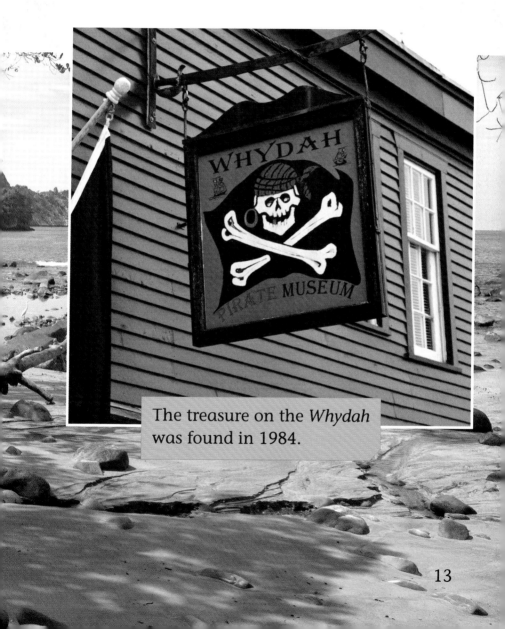

The treasure on the *Whydah* was found in 1984.

Are there really tomb robbers?

Some Ancient **tombs** and graves contain lots of treasure. Important and rich people often had precious coins, jewellery and objects buried with them.

In Ancient Egypt, tomb robbers often worked in gangs. Experts believe the tomb of King Tutankhamun was robbed twice before it was opened in 1922.

The young king's tomb was raided soon after his funeral, but the tomb robbers didn't take all the treasure.

Tomb robbers are still active today. In **Guatemala**, archaeologists excavating an important Maya site discovered over 100 tunnels dug into the sides of stone temples by looters.

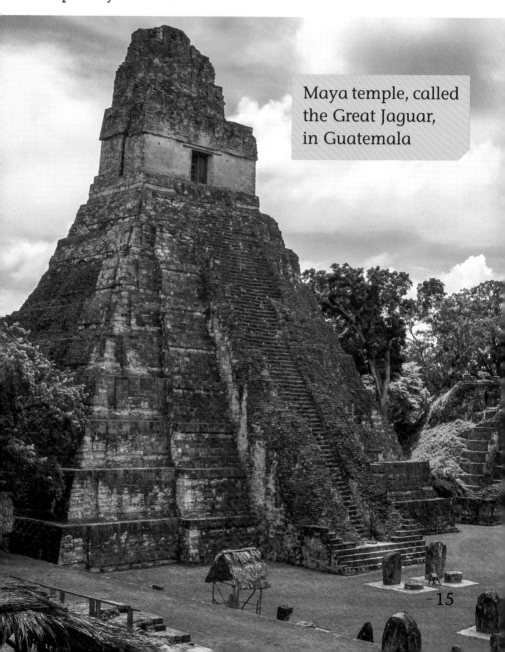

Maya temple, called the Great Jaguar, in Guatemala

What other kinds of treasure are there?

Finding treasure isn't just about what it's worth. Often, objects have important cultural value.

For Native Americans, belts and headdresses decorated with prized natural materials, like eagle feathers and cowrie or wampum shells, are treasure.

In many cultures, helmets, shields and swords are treasured for their age, precious materials and craftmanship.

Native American headdress from the 19th century

The Battersea Shield. This Iron Age shield is over 2,000 years old.

a replica of an Anglo-Saxon helmet from Sutton Hoo in Suffolk, UK

Can you keep the treasure you find?

Treasure hunters must get permission
from the landowner to search on their
land and report any treasure they find.
If you find something important,
you may not be able to keep it,
but it could be of historical importance!

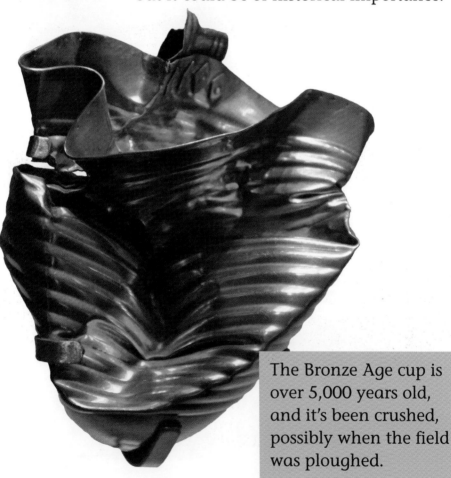

The Bronze Age cup is
over 5,000 years old,
and it's been crushed,
possibly when the field
was ploughed.

In 2001, a metal detectorist found a gold Bronze Age cup in a field in Kent, UK. The British Museum bought the cup and put it on display.

In 2009, a metal detectorist discovered a hoard of Iron Age **torcs** in a field in Scotland. Important finds are often bought by museums so the public can enjoy learning about them.

This 2,000-year-old gold torc was worn around the neck.

Are there any lost treasures?

There are many legends of lost treasures. King John's treasure, including his crown jewels, gold and money, is said to have been lost in 1216 somewhere in the Fens in East Anglia, UK. Historians are still looking for it today.

The Amber Room was made for a **Prussian** king in the 18th century. Its walls were decorated with **amber** panels, backed with gold leaf. It was looted during the Second World War and may have been destroyed by bombing.

The Amber Room was in the Catherine Palace, St Petersburg, Russia. This reconstruction shows what it would have looked like.

Are there any treasure-finding gadgets?

In the past, treasure hunters used maps,
compasses and shovels. Today, alongside
metal detectors, archaeologists
use lots of gadgets to help them.

Drones can carry remote sensors to scan larger areas, and artificial satellite images help treasure hunters study the land.

Artificial satellites can detect objects underground using sonar (sound waves) or radar (radio waves).

Are there any treasure hunts today?

Some people set up treasure hunts as challenges, with the treasure as a reward. They plant clues in a poem, painting or even on a mobile phone app.

Geocaching is an outdoor treasure hunt using **GPS** on smartphones or tablets. When you find the geocache, there is a logbook inside to sign and there may be a trinket too, but you must put it back or replace it.

An artist published a picture book called *Masquerade* in 1979. The pictures contained hidden clues to the location of a jewelled golden hare.

The gold hare was made by the artist, Kit Williams. Its hiding place was discovered in 1982.

Can anyone become a treasure hunter?

Yes, they can. Beachcombing is a good way to hunt for treasures washed up by the waves. All you have to do is walk along a beach and search!

As long as you are safe and respect the land, treasure is all around us, just waiting to be found!

a 500-year-old coin found by the River Thames, UK

So, there really is buried treasure!

27

Glossary

aerial seen from the air

amber a yellowy fossilized tree resin used for jewellery

Angles people from Germanic Europe who invaded and settled in Britain in the 5th century

archaeologists people who study the history of humans by looking at ancient objects people have left behind

artificial satellite machines sent into space to orbit a planet and send back data

GPS global positioning system, which uses radio signals to give locations and directions

Guatemala a country in Central America

historical famous or important in history

hoard a large amount

occupied lived in as rulers

Prussian belonging to a region in Northern Europe once ruled as a German Kingdom

raiders people who suddenly attack to steal things

tombs large rooms, sometimes underground, where people bury the dead

torcs neck ornaments made from twisted, often precious, metal

troves collections of valuable things

Index

Treasure!

gold and silver coins

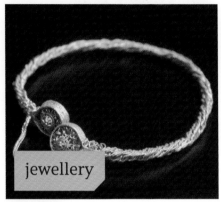

jewellery

helmets

shields

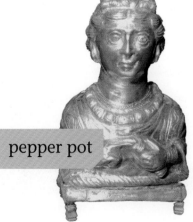

pepper pot

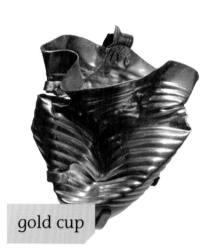
gold cup

headdress

gold hare

Ancient Egyptian mask

Amber Room

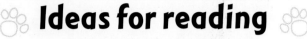

Ideas for reading

Written by Christine Whitney
Primary Literacy Consultant

Reading objectives:
- retrieve information from non-fiction
- be introduced to non-fiction books that are structured in different ways
- explain and discuss their understanding of books

Spoken language objectives:
- ask relevant questions
- speculate, imagine and explore ideas through talk
- participate in discussions

Curriculum links: History: Develop an awareness of the past; Writing: Write for different purposes

Word count: 1250

Interest words: troves, hoard, tomb, raiders, archaeologist, beachcombing

Build a context for reading

- Ask children what they understand by the word *treasure*. Have they ever been on a treasure hunt?
- Read the title of the book and ask children to discuss this question. What do they expect to read about in this book?
- Encourage children to ask three questions about buried treasure. Check for answers when reading the book.

Understand and apply reading strategies

- Read up to page 5 together and ask children to explain to each other what they understand about the meaning of the word *treasure*.
- Continue to read to page 11. Ask children to summarise the different ways people find buried treasure.
- Ask children to find two lost treasure troves mentioned on pages 20 and 21.
- Ask children to explain the use of the contents page. Suggest that they ask each other for the page number where they might find the answer to this question: *Can anyone become a treasure hunter?*
- Look closely at the index. What does it tell the reader? How is this different from the contents page?